Matter of Fact

Other Books by Eamon Grennan

POETRY

What Light There Is & Other Poems

As If It Matters

So It Goes

Relations:
New & Selected Poems

Still Life with Waterfall

The Quick of It

TRANSLATION

Leopardi: Selected Poems

Oedipus at Colonus
(with Rachel Kitzinger)

ESSAYS

Facing the Music:
Irish Poetry in the Twentieth Century

Matter of Fact

Eamon Grennan

Graywolf Press
SAINT PAUL, MINNESOTA

Publication of this volume is made possible in part by a grant provided by the Minnesota State Arts Board, through an appropriation by the Minnesota State Legislature; a grant from the Wells Fargo Foundation Minnesota; and a grant from the National Endowment for the Arts, which believes that a great nation deserves great art. Significant support has also been provided by the Bush Foundation; Target; the McKnight Foundation; and other generous contributions from foundations, corporations, and individuals. To these organizations and individuals we offer our heartfelt thanks.

Published by Graywolf Press
2402 University Avenue, Suite 203
Saint Paul, Minnesota 55114

www.graywolfpress.org

Published in the United States of America

ISBN 978-1-55597-500-5

2 4 6 8 9 7 5 3 1
First Graywolf Printing, 2008

Library of Congress Control Number: 2007940214

Cover design: Jeenee Lee Design

Cover art: Adriaen Coorte (Dutch, ca. 1660–after 1707). *Gooseberries on a Table,* 1701. Oil on paper mounted on wood; 29.7 x 22.8 cm.

Acknowledgments

Grateful thanks to the editors of the following magazines, where many of these poems, in earlier versions, first appeared.

AGNI: "Edge," "On Change *(From the Train)*" [as "From the Train"]

Bat City Review: "On Change *(Body Language)*," "Hawklight 2" [as "Hawk Entering Hemlock"]

Bloomsday (2004): "Soundings" [as "Spring Riff"]

Clifden Anthology: "Opposing Forces"

Field: "Rome, the Pantheon" [as "Roman Sights"]

Five Points: "The Curve," "Intermission," "Simple Pleasures"

The Gettysburg Review: "Turtle and Two Girls"

The Georgia Review: "Hawklight 3" [as "Twentieth Anniversary"]

The Hudson Review: "Solitary"

Image: "Cold Comfort" [as "Tasting the Snow"]

The Irish Times: "In Venice on My Father's Anniversary," "What It Is," "Cézanne and Family," "City Dusk"

The Kenyon Review: "Night," "Start of March, Connemara," "In Bits"

Literary Imagination: "Meteor Shower, Long Beach Island"

The New Republic: "With Flowers and Curtain"

The New Yorker: "Steady Now," "A Few Facts"

On Earth: "Drained Lake, Heron in Mud"

The Ontario Review: "April Note" [as "It"]

Orion: "Bee Fuchsia"

Poetry: "Signland," "And So On" [as "After Violence"], "Beholding the Hare"

Poetry Ireland Review: "Trees in Time"

Poetry London: "Hawklight 1" [as "March Hawk"], "Going Gone," "Wildflowers in a Glass of Water," "Ladybird and Mother"

A Public Space: "Steam in Sunlight," last part of "Look Out" [as "Knowledge"]

Riverine: "Something," "Innocence of Things"

Salamander: "Like" [as "At Parting"]
Salmagundi: "Goldcrest"
The Seneca Review: "A Thrush by Utamaro"
Shenandoah: "Foam," "Nervous System, 2" [as "Why Goodbye"]
The Stinging Fly: "Another Country *(Wardrobe)*" [as "Parents' Wardrobe"], "Darkling Blues *(August)*" [as "Where Things Touch"]
The Threepenny Review: "The Search"
TriQuarterly: "Darkling Blues *(December)*" [as "Lying Awake"]
The Yale Review: "Of Space and Skin" [as "Riff of Space and Skin"]

"The Curve" was published in *The Best American Poetry 2006,* and "The Search" was published in *The Best of Irish Poetry 2007*.

Contents

Something spoke into stillness, something was silent,
something went its way.

PAUL CELAN, "Cologne, at the Station"

A pack of cards is falling toward the floor.
The sun is secretly shining on a wall.
One remembers a woman standing in such a dress.

WALLACE STEVENS, "The Bouquet"

I

Start of March, Connemara

(In memory of Elizabeth Bishop)

The wind colder even than March in Maine, though the same sea
is your greens of mutton-fat jade and bleached artichoke,
the water thumbed, wind-scumbled, its heroic white manes
blown to bits at the shoreline. Two white gulls, wing-tilted,
are surfing the sou'wester. How do they do it, finding the right
angle in the gale and—angels of the shiverblast—adapting to it,
letting it take them the way they're going?

A lone cormorant
blackly flashes, heading west like a messenger. Breasting
the choppy wave-peaks, he's all purpose and intensity, plunging
headlong into his own unknown future, reaching out to it
without a thought, while I go back the way I came
along wet sand that's glistening with relief, my own prints
erased already, *writ in water.*

Rock and water have to be
our elements here, and today's buffeting air—which these
rain-plovers pay no mind to, a little tribe rising as one, spinning
into the wind, whistling their shrill excitement in flight: glitterwings
making their mark against green gape-water, then gone.

Nervous System

1.

The word *prayer* is gone—twig in the wind,
winter light, one tawny leaf starched
to a spectre of itself on old snow, a late
beckoning. Indoors it's silence—or not silence
but something like the presence of *withdrawal,*

what any glass or pewter vessel might feel
with the air drawn out of it—some sort of
vacuum, only thicker, like staring at a sheet
of antique paper and seeing the watermark
in its corner (anchor, she-wolf, horned head

of Artemis) no longer floats, a ghost, there.
So absence (the weight of it, the way air
pulses, the phantom limb keeps throbbing)
is a *something out there,* not dead stuff
blank against the window. An opening, or almost.

2.

Rilke's *petrified rage* can't be the answer. Something
swims in the bloodstream, some impossible-to-detect-
till-it-has-done-its-work venom. High up between blue
and branches a grey-haired man in a cherry-picker

will step out into the maple sky and hang himself there
and dangle, cutting what's redundant. No knowing
what might happen if you move into the open like that,
a show to any jealous eye. Such flirtatious outrage,

not even the Angel sees where the smile is going—
so why not shuffle off, unshriven, into transparent air
and count the days, placing the envelope of secrets

where the saucer of nutmeg was? For even now a goldfinch
lights out of the cat's mouth, every yellow squawk of it
saved and sudden into the rest of its life, not looking back.

What It Is

It is in the smallest leaf—of oak, maple, elm, dogwood, birch
or Chinese redwood. In the way leaves droop in the air
of this rain-laundered time of day, each involuntary drip
a pearl-drop earring. Shadows of barn gable and pin-oak tree
live in print on the avocado green of grass. What it is

is that *Amen* stuck in Macbeth's throat, or the road one
wheatear didn't take, or the child you didn't have the right
time or space to have, all its dark-eyed answers—eyes
glittering behind each twig of the persimmon, fleshlights
igniting every fruitglobe. What it is is ripening, so

inhale the immaculate late afternoon as you pass
through the garden: fruit, dust, moist fungus, a fine distillate
of finality you keep breathing, being in your own way
a part of it, wanting its laden air to leaven your lungs,
letting the heart be a small box of beaten gold that holds

secrets and hopeless promises. It is rife with promise.

Wintermouth

Even the column of steam from the powerhouse chimney
is ashen gold this morning. *Tormented and melodious,*

someone said of Celan, the way the robins were yesterday
in their flutterjazz between branches. Now all is shadow

or blind white: world wears a second skin, keeps itself
at the point of freezing. To feel at times like this,

the way the stream might feel when ice bites deep
and deeper: gradual contraction of everything

to one solid slab of irremediable cold. Only, deep down,
there's an underneath, and down there, chill as it is, water

is still moving, blind mouths ease through and taste
their own blood pulsing, that trim little engine the heart

re-beating its sound-life, going on in the cold. To let
this tongue inch out: tasting air; testing the element.

Like

Like that feral black hat on Vermeer's cavalier (a panther
prowling the parlour where the girl sits smiling
into the eyes of departure); like that rustling in the bushes

where the child sees a dream of pointed teeth flashing
for wolf-fox, bear-cat, anything, a blaze of yellow eyes;
like the sense that softens your bones as you step out

on a stretch of ice, imagining its fragility, its depths of dark,
and how wet cold would close over your breath, your ears
drown in the sound of singing sheet-ice, the high-pitched

moan of its fracturing; like any minute of innocent sunlight
suddenly ruptured, ransacked by blackout—this hysteria
of nearness keeps my head on the edge of flying to bits

through the window in particles of light, millions of them
winging it like all lost causes, like something off by heart.

Look Out

This morning it's our bare, moist, muscular masters, the trees, that have to stand in shadowy majesty for something. No stopping the colourstuff in pussy willows, or what happens to any stem this weather reddens, thickens, fills with only its own happening.

The needle pumping nothing through your tongue but pristine numbness has you waking around mid-day, sun blazing, dumb as a fish being filleted for tomorrow's dinner—not sole on the bone but some slow simmered thing that leaches all its life-juices out and sets them one against the other, to teach you again how in the end good ends depend on death to begin with.

Turning the other cheek is not the answer: didn't the shadow of the turkey vulture—itself a black shadow stapled to the blank blue sky-face—only yesterday cross the path you were tracing, and didn't your blood skitter for an instant, sensing its thwart and pitiless intention?

But could words like *relish, savour,* or *abide* strike a right note to end on? Now clouds are brazen radiance, are scarcely matter—only thick light, white brilliance against blue. Later they'll grow a heart-fraught leaden grey, day dimming—though a still fierce gleam to the west makes one small nimbus melting in the blue, transfiguring birches and leftover snow to this deep, meditative rose.

Another time it's a word like *roofbeam* brings you out of emptiness: you picture the nestle of it, light smearing its grain, the long silence before sleep, your father finding a fresh unclouded residence in the offing—a sort of guardian, different but reliable.

Then sleep makes a clean sweep of things, the ceiling of your head a crown of stars, their names unknown, a realm away from impermanence—though that's your main address now, the word *home* cropping up only here and there. Because—as the maker of mists remarked that first morning—*Love is not consolation, it is light.*

Injunction

Needles of rain. Ground makes no moan.
Wind-sigh in the sycamore. What's passing.
Haw berries rusting the hawthorn hedges.

Don't look back. Think Orpheus. Pillar of salt.
One breath, then another. Sweat of apprehension.
Still life with wind and breadcrumbs.

But I keep wanting to turn around.
No whimsy in it, staggering the gamut
bright red. And as deadly, she said, as nightshade.

Still you went on. Looking at her lips.
Sea verge to cliff edge, no shaking off
what shadows you. Seeing that

rain-swollen torrent at Gurteen,
you wanted to give yourself over
to its foamy, stone-broken dissolution

of salt. *And then?* What's not, she said,
possible. Or was it a question?
Even this rocky crevice

where the wren is nesting.

Trees in Time

The trees we've walked in shade between
lay, a week or so ago, disbranched, flat out,
stiff as boards beneath unmediated light, naked
to the next phase of their humiliation,

which happened yesterday, so this morning
they're no more than mounds of woodchips
gleaming a faint fleshgleam in morning light,
a diaphanous wreath of steam winding from

the peak of each as if a blind volcanic heart
were buried there, still smouldering, being
the trees' last gasp of resin-scented breath
entering the world I pass through

pondering what happens to wholeness—
how it breaks down until it's
only air, yet giving up still this sweetness
or bittersweet *thickness* which I'm struck

to silence by, and stand in, listening.

Solitary

In the photo a scarf and the edge of a white sweater keep her breast from sight. Face and tumbled hair candid as any patch of blue through cloud. Against a blue backdrop, two swallows kiss on the wing, belly to white-as-cloudshine belly. On the window ledge a blackbird, sleek as a new-polished shoe. Between the off-beat tick of two clocks time passes. Outside, a plump bird with peach-coloured chest feeds grass-seeds to its squeaking youngster. From the mantelpiece his own three young ones smile: Rome railway station—they go their separate ways. Migrant and scattershot, between nostalgia and anticipation, they're a hearsay of light and lumpish matter stumbling in tongues, a happenstance flashing along the rim of the blackbird's corn-kernel beak as it snaps fast on a morsel of crust.

What he keeps in mind mostly are moments of meeting and going away: glimpses of coming together, then turning away in sleep. Or at stations, airports, a buoyancy of expectation, then the leaning in at last to each other's faces, hands trying to hold back the hands of the clock; time spreading itself like salt in the warm wound. He feels the wind now, sees under its measureless tread the dock leaves wagging dumb green tongues. Rain swirls its platinum smoke across the tattered garden, and he notes near the window a spider killing a fly, the pure ferocious *matter* of the act and then such patience: that lying on top like a sturdy lover, wings veined and transparent, despair in their blurry whirl, their terminal buzzing. Now killed and killer seem at peace, sleeping together, their clean body-work done, only one of them dreaming. Like a tiny *pietà*, the fly reclines in the spider's tidy embrace, and it's finished.

In Venice on My Father's Anniversary

When the long boat stopped in the dark
where I stood among the pillars of the old fish market,
I hesitated till it was loaded with souls
who stood for the crossing, then let them go—
each pressing a coin into the hand of the boatman
whose breathing I could hear and the splash of his oars
when he turned the craft and ferried over the dark stream
that small troop of voyagers. But when
the boat came back a second time
I too stepped in with those waiting
and handed over my obol and took my stand with care
so the vessel wouldn't shake or waver. Then I felt
the night air and the breath of air off water
swaddle me, and heard only the in and out of oars,
and felt the water shaking under us where we stood
in the bodies we had. But
when we stepped ashore on the other side
into what I thought would be strangeness,
I find myself in the place I'd just left
and start walking the known track once more.

Wing and Prayer

Haze for days. Rowanberries darkening to brown. Birds falling from branches under a lukewarm, almost African rain. When the dove becomes a handful of feathers flying from car-wheels, I call up again that man of cardboard—face in hands, crying in a corner, the window squinnying in at him—and find no song to brighten the heartbreak-grey of the vacant kitchen or kindle a spark in the darkened fire-grate; and even those roses, light-blown as they are, will die in the abandoned living-room of thirst. But if I lift my eyes a moment, might I find in a flail of nerves and marrowchill the fruit-dish mounded with clementines, altars everywhere, and even in this dingy underground a flower shop shining near midnight, a goldfinch lighting up its bush in icy weather, or the dreamfox disappearing into the house of childhood—henna flash then gone—with its pale ginger head, its eye an ember flaring?

At dusk, then, to be dazzled by Venus and Jupiter in conjunction, gold of whiskey, doorknobs' gilt or glass, or how the fact of faces grows stranger and stranger: faint puce browns, steely greys, the range of ivory, rose, biscuit, one faint shade of plum. And the ocean roaring on its short leash, a lone gull riding the gale bareback, balancing on its bill a single blink of salted light. Given such, no wonder I have to close my eyes to all the mirrors, shut my ears to the wren cockcrowing its hurlyburly, composing a home among the garage clutter. Or *start like a guilty thing surprised* from the hue and cry of kitchen habits: innocent clatter of forks and stainless steel knives falling from dry hands into a drawer; silence of the stove; the oven a dark patience for the heart to come on. Knowing only the *broken white* of a dress and its bone-coloured buttons, two arms stretching sleeveless out of it.

In Passing

It could be the glide and slide of traffic
over wet streets—funereal, with headlights on—
or some more minute distraction, looking
for the woodpecker on a bare branch: black and white
plume-braid, scarlet head, indefatigable beak.

Or seeing in this frigid February morning
the brief love affair that great burst of steam
funneling from the powerhouse valve
and exploding in a huge white bloom of cloud
has with the frozen air.

Brevity! Brevity! the heart cries
at the whole roiling mass melting in no time
to a few white wisps curling away: nothing
to them, yet nothing in this grey morning
is as bright as they are.

Innocence of Things

Driving north. Shivers of valediction.
Tweed-folds of the Catskills in abrasive light;
risen flame of a redtail riding a thermal;
two geese through blue immensity. Sun

scribbles its calligraphy of angle-spines
and snag-arms. All the dead leaves
up again, jigging and reeling from
this brash wind scatter. The barred

tail of a raccoon shimmers a little
in breeze-flutter. Rest of him sprawled
still as stone on the road's shoulder.
Drip of fresh meltwater off a snowbank

is the tick of the clock this March day
moves to, slow as moss-ooze. Brazen
daylight; acres of snow under a sky
of sapphire; and I'm remembering

my old friend's fine old hands
as she held the fork steady, snail-slow,
tendering a curl of baby corn
to her mouth, and I want to set her

next to the innocence of things
as they stand up in frailty and fortitude
to light, and take its daily measure—
their secular selves singular and glowing.

(In memory of Phoebe Palmer)

Soundings

On the astral plane! she said. Heaven forbid. Fleshless, beyond even
body heat, what would be left to matter? Now here out of nowhere
shoot these sudden shoots of wild onion, sharp green in the eye, green
pungency in the nose, and this watery, edgy, sidling disappearance

of green at tongue tip. Item: the way the light falls till it hits something
upright and stops there, casting spindle-shadows—the great white birch
in my neighbours' garden, say, that simply stands there, rapt
and letting it happen, though this can't help my old friend, who's gone

from curiosity about change in the configuration of clouds
over the years, to pure scare, her breath coming in small spoonfuls,
hardly enough to trouble the cooling air. Here now the musical chuckle
the American robin shares with his cousin the Irish blackbird

scales the morning, and where there was yesterday only one
brown nuthatch chittering among sunflower seeds on my windowsill
now there are two, one either end of the feeder, where they peck
a seed apiece then look at each other a split second, then gone, each

a slight tan glow in going. I find myself sounding such things out
by skin-instinct or some sort of soul-braille, I suppose, spirit-fingers
flickering to take all in. When the clouds are broken, sudden
shards of blue porcelain smile down at us, offering reassurance

the way glintbits of shattered cups and saucers might, come to light
in our first garden. But what leaks out is something else: one more
passing-bell of recognition rousing the molecules of desire, unsettled
by smells of fresh paint, new carpet freshly laid. One sharp

particle at a time you take it in: *Newness is all,* you hear it sigh to itself
in its tongue of melancholy illuminations, bringing instances to light
of possibility or resignation, each carried home like a low moan
in April's leafage. *Listen, you could live here: everything's to happen.*

City Dusk

Next door to the video store and the tattoo artist, under
the rattle and thrum of rush-hour summer traffic
that paces day with bells, horns, sirens, you'll stay
among rooms your nerves are getting used to: light

comes in without knocking, remains till after nine,
leaving its shadow-selves six stories down and
pottering under plane trees towards that park bench
among bottles and long overcoats, listening

to the Litany of Our Lady of Misfortune: *Shadow of*
stumbling mothers, pray for us. Shadow of crumbled wits,
pray for us. From this window, watch evening
fray slow to rose tatters, rags of cloud, a whisper

of mint green suddenly coming through. Soon
the time for words will lay its cool fingers to the skin
of your neck and waken the warm there, so you'll rise
as though from a dream, and find the room empty.

Darkling Blues

(August)
Shapes of small stones on the gravel drive, each at an angle to its companions: lines of shadow lying between them, zigzags of dark tying their brights together. We've lain like that. Between limbs where they're touching there is—dividing skin from skin—this shadow-line: what painters see and settle their still lifes by, each object a world to itself. Which is why we go into each other with tongues and fingers, mouth to mouth, part into part—trying to erase the line between any two in the world, between even these bodies startled for fleeing seconds into being each other: blind, involuntary and dispersed as a breeze among sycamore leaves. Last night a clean moon in the polished, dust-blue sky; tide-pools at Omey a gleamy rose. But to be driving home through patches of ground fog, on the border where sea had eaten by jagged degrees into land, was to keep crossing the line from clarity to blindness back to clear sight again. Hedge-loom of green and scarlet. Hands gripping the wheel; eyes peering through a muddle-mesh of landmarks and mist. Meadowsweet's undulant, creamy surf. Light leaping, a wild thing, in the dark.

(December)
Night thoughts pin him to glittershapes on the curtains: fallen leaves caught in their last incarnate colours. The fabric ghost-white. At the slightest breath a slow, spectral motion. His dream a monumental skeleton of metal: raw light crucifies a few spars of leftover scaffolding. Scattered at its foot are kettle, bed, toys, the kitchen dishes; chenille scarf, silver breast-brooch, amber necklace; a gold and lapis lazuli bracelet, its freckled deep blue hoarding light. Soon he'll hear small birds on the feeder or the hawk's high-up screaming—a broadwing blazon, ginger-tailed, on cloud that winter's turned the colour of canvas, weather-yellowed.

Of Space and Skin

Profligate, astonishing, the air a green curtain
glinting with seeds that flicker falling, that spin
and spin, dibbling into their next life of either
all is over or *What's this? blind roots? a burrowing?*

You take your pick and make your hopeful choice:
whatever happens, it's a place you know
you've got to make the most of, though the shapes
you've grown accustomed to are husks and tatters.

But peering out at the river now, its white blobs
and bobbers on the water, you see space integrated
and put to good use—as you would be, and not
in splintered bits, watching out of gouged eyes

the mourning doves flutter up from weeds
and reeds and grass to light on branches, begin
to moan in chorus there while spring's prim
lushness softens the small hills. Still

in hiding, sidling from one skulking-place
to another, you wonder what name this game has
and if you'll return to the world of ordinary footsteps,
to the many amazing ways skin has (sewn

seamless over bone) of being skin—the pungent
wonder it offers your eyes on West Broadway:
bazaar of blazing shades; riverrun of hungry glances;
eye-flying fingers, neck curves, nude shoulders.

Another Week with Hölderlin

But where is the man
Who can remain free
His whole life long, alone
Doing his heart's desire?

Monday

Woods a green blaze; smoke off the lake. River-bowl of burning light. To be on, as he says, *roads travelers take.* World a wall of fire, boundaries between this and that eliding like light off harried water. In the underground, smears of firelight glisten at first from rusted tracks until—blind as beetles hearing the agony of shunt and wheel-shaft, the grind, the groaning—we start hauling the huge intractable weight of our *(what's the word?)* along with us.

Tuesday

In the city I lose one thing after another: the car, my glasses, the house I've passed the evening in with friends, the friends. Entering the cathedral, I descend with two or three strangers to the crypt and we close the heavy door. We pull the bell-ropes anchored there. We spin the pulleys working the bells. Up as high in the tower as I can see, one bell then another starts swinging, ringing. Belling, we pull, we spin, shaking ancient walls. The ground's raw earth knobbled with stone and, barred behind us, the door. We're bound to this—to filling the world with sound. *Likewise,* he says, *mourning is in error.* Still no one comes.

Wednesday

The Grand Canal near Portobello Bridge. Light shaping itself in the wake that one duck makes on murky water. The place Italian, almost, as sunshine. Sun-disk shattering on the mallard's stippled shadow. Folds of the Fates in Stephen's Green. *But desire,* he says, *is foolish in the face of fate.*

On pitiless patches of grass the girls clutch at the boys, and the boys in their panic of pride clutch back. And grapple to them, looking away.

Thursday

Whose head, neat as a hinged lid, lifts just above the eyebrows? Floats in a flood of sudden commuters flailing across the station hall? I fumble in one face after another. Whose two eyes stab with *I miss you more than I can say*? The heart, blood thumping, comes into leaf, feels the heat. How it licks and nibbles. A bite of something like surprise. *Often when you've barely given it a thought,* he says, *it just happens.*

Friday

Spirit or not, he says, one *must keep to the world,* so you are grass coming up from under the long sleep of snow, every touch of colour bleached out, and you lie there, feeling nothing but the weight lifted that's buried you for months, letting the good air get to you with its hundred subtleties of touch, its promise of something happening at last, even a breeze strengthening to storm, a rasp of dead leaves, scouring hail, the way rain drills deep its glitter-fingers. Flesh, then: its kinetic harking after something headlong and lighthearted as the weather shifts and air becomes a spectrum of blues you can see through—no one of them going to waste.

Saturday

The Pissarros have became dimensional again, so you enter and are at home in one of their empty houses, the one framed in a cage of birches at a blind corner. *Someone reach me,* he says, *a cupful of dark light,* so you stand under a spilling gutter, see fat fire-water splashing, feel the quick-bright lick of tongues, so your bare head burns and your neck glints and shivers, as if you'd happened to stand in the way of a blessing otherwise intended. It lucidates you, moving to its proper end—lodging there, still quivering.

Sunday

You watch the deer stepping downhill to the pond: a mother and two young, they pace graceful and steady, looking about. You're in the presence—*near,* he says, *and hard to grasp*—and try to remember the lilies of the field, the transparent air you're up against. It is a sort of start: a faint thing, but like the smell of blood and its taste in your mouth, salt-sweet.

With Flowers and Curtain

Like lilies you imagine in the vestibule of Hell
these tall nameless flowers in front of the library

are straight talkers, blazing their rhetoric of *stare*
and *go away,* huge scarlet vowels setting minds on fire

with thoughts of furnace sex: to be just burned up
and no release. Is there no way to close your eyes

to such feral, fiery erections, shut out the sight
and not panic? Though your dreams are blood-soaked,

you wake dry as a bone to watch the bedroom curtain
dancing, its bulge and bellying and sudden intakes

making a waist, a hip, a hot flank on the go, an opening—
though you know it's only the wind getting wind of things

and leading its shaky life in any pliable, light, near-
alive object. But what body language it has:

no loop repeated, no gesture wasted, every shiver
melting into a next quickening shudder, the next

astonished full stop. Pause—then the garbage truck
is grinding the early hour into a hash of crashes, a clamour

of metal, glass, recyclable plastic. Wrenched towards
day-state by the woeful din of it, you have to think

how by the darkened library those flowers are burning
to a stalk; while the curtain, you see, is still dancing.

April Note

From a bare branch the kestrel streaks across my evening walk,
catching a splash of late sun for a second on its tawny back
and that's that as it disappears between trees already in shadow
and I walk to the dead end of McCracken Lane, to a small
iron gate I lock behind me, that *Dead End* edgy in my head
till I hear the birds—who ignore our signs—rejoice in the later
and later light, a wonder they know only as the way things are,

and I remember hearing, early this morning, the kestrel's wild cry
and seeing finches and starlings cower on a weathercock, bluejays
in the naked heart of the maple fall silent, two Canada geese
wind-sail over on their way north. Wondering what isn't taking off,
lighting out, embracing change, I turn to the pussywillows'
breath of yellow, to let it stand as a blessing to the transient eye—
an infant promise left *without more mercy to its own protection*
and favour of the climate. It's a small bundle only, but of breathing.

Foam

These phoebes contrive their household
where they can. Year after year
they're back, seeking the right spot

for a lodging, each under-bridge taken over,
underscoring in their buoyant perpetuity
your own Chagall fantasy of flying

through high windows and feeling
how the free air feels, seeing
the neon-green dawn-screech

of skunk cabbage. Ducks and geese
light out, starting over elsewhere
easy. But you are light and shade,

seeking day to clouded day
some reconciling, and if you go on
like this you'll be apprehended

carrying anniversary balloons,
their painted roses. The soul, you see,
is a sort of salmon, a rose-red swimmer

in the sea of self, though any
second now you may find yourself
in the *quantum vacuum,* that *seethe of being*

that is, again, the nest
of possibility, though now, wherever you look,
there's only foam, which here

in this little room is what we're making
of ourselves, the ground
under our feet grown centrifugal

and a damp unruly light
proffering—through colours of
mud, sand, ash—its own luminous moment.

II

Steam in Sunlight

So start with sex: the sight of birds at seed,
their urgency a sequin of fire in tiny eyes—
and in mine too, maybe, as I burrow in,
an eel of hot intentions, a wheel
of give and take, a whole cascade of hope
before that ache of restoration to the world
as is, history in all its homely features
and the hour later than we think, footsteps
measuring the way the child enters, tentative,
and slides between us.

So then we three
are peeling clementines and the day starts
closing over my head, till I catch nothing
but its racket of traffic, loud voices
muffled, my own words sunk like stones
stuck in the under-mud.

Bundled back
into the body-suit, shackled to the tick
of heart-clocks, I call back the steam I saw
in sunlight after my shower, the bathroom
a tankful of molecular grey radiance
staining the world with its own infinite,
instant-by-glittering-instant, quick
play of starting over, the road open.

Night

But what to make of night, then, its caul of stars crystal-riveted, yet—for all their fixture—unsteady as breath, able to be winked out by the smallest cloud? Night scratched at by traffic, a chirrup or two from tree-frog or dark-flitting bird. Night with a dash of cut grass, parched earth, the skunk that gave his life to the blind hunger of trucks thundering up Main Street, an aftermath tainting our air so we won't forget his wild passage nor how we caught him short between one safe hedgerow and another, left his ebony and vanilla body tucked into itself beyond all remedy at the edge of the road, gathering the risen, all-enshrouding dust.

Our cats know night for what it is—a dark, skinless beast with blazing eyes, a mouth soft as sleep but open to swallow their ambition, a gigantic companion they can lie beside, the one who covers for them and out of whose shadow they spring to bring the little infant of night—fieldmouse or streaked chipmunk—in their teeth, inhaling its last horizontal high-pitched cry: *Oh mother it's too late!*

Now night: last notes before the daughter of the house calls it a day, closes her music, goes to bed, so when the father gets home he'll find the hall door locked and a note in an unknown hand pinned to the lintel: *Night comes down. Nothing to be done. Try again. Keep trying.* He looks around.

Meteor Shower, Long Beach Island

Coming into its shining own, the barest crescent of a moon
gimlets its pinpoint through light that's blanched cranberry
and peach, as dusk sifts in and settles around us so everything
is glimmer and glisten, is glow. Walking away we keep turning back,

trying to say what colours we can see, turning till all is only
evening blue, a radioactive stone, and in it the platinum sliver
of the moon. We strain to take in this distant wonder, desperate
to hold it as we walk away, even as we see ourselves

become silhouettes in our own safe-keeping. Deep night then,
and then a pre-dawn sky, stars in their shape-up constellations, sudden
light-smears streaking the dark. Explosions of illuminated dust,
the miracle happening over our heads where we lie on sand

looking up at purblind blackness ripped by daubs or sudden falls
of cosmic glitter, each gone before we can say *There!* So we keep watch,
flat on the sand like that, the place windless and mild and silent
except for the slap of surf, the soft cries of awe crying *Look!*

Hawklight

1.

Hungry season. Hawk, redtail, lights a vacant maple:
brain one continuous shivery nail-rasp, scorching eyes
to ash. Small birds on the alert, air cacophonous

with scales and prattlings. Hawk throws head about:
readiness is all, all solitude and manic appetite. Stand-by
in silhouette, figuring such verbs as *Want! Be-here!*

Stopped, you'll see the sudden tilt of his gingery
black head, quick blink of an eye in which you'd spot
yellow iris, pupil black as soot, the moonless void

of lethal patience that knows *when-where* to strike
once in an explosion of bones and tiny eyes
brimming with blood, a cry swallowed, a breath

quenched—earthbound or native to the air. Another day
goes by, survived: hawkvoice moves up a notch,
filing sky to wildness: sharp ravel-song splaying entrails.

2.

Sudden, a plummet, the marsh hawk enters a hemlock
and stands, steadying himself, stopped not far from
my head, on a branch too thick to shake or sway much

so I can see the hook of his beak and the livid black
and yellow target-circles of the eye he turns on me—
a laser graiping my grounded bulk into the meltdown

his brain is. Stays there out of the crows' way
that heckle, harass: alert to every twig-snap, footstep
and the strung silence into which a squirrel's just crept

with stuttering pulse, to shiver there, sheltering. So
I learn how heart heaves, how flexed muscle keeps
leashing, unleashing in a book of feathers, how tongue

hisses *hawkstand! squirrelshiver! crowclamour! now!*

3.
Only when the day was well on its way to extinction, rain
closing in, sponging the picture with muddy light, did I turn
to what I knew was lodged at its heart or in its throat
like a fishbone, a glottal-stop splinter of mackerel scratching
the soft bed of my mouth. I'd been wondering if it was

something in the air—a smell of fresh blood or some small thing
ripe for slaughter—that had the evening full of hawks, two
of them then three flying to a low branch near me. Their sawtooth
screams, then twenty years gone like a shot and I'm standing
by my father's last breath again, dumbed by sudden absence

and no answering. But when I look up now—his anniversary
weight loading my shoulders—I see the mist is rising, raising
its pale greylight off softening snow, and it's as if the whole
sober earth were all of a sudden a flurry, a fizz of spirits.

Breath

Small paws in leafmatter. Smell of resin and balsam filling me for a minute
before I go. All that's alive in this necropolis of wanwood and woodchip
is the scent of what was locked deep in leaf-vein and the grain of things

when the woods were walk-through and see-about, where now two squirrels
swirl skittering up peeled treebark. To stop in the middle of it all, the after-
noon light informing each crevice of bark, each filament in the squirrel's tail,

or gilding every mint-green smear of lichen, or falling like a tongue of fire
on a skyblue plastic canister—is to stand inside the pharmacopoeia of aromas
exhaled by mounds of rot, their airy liberated nothings become something

like that evidence of the world which I saw this morning in the small
bursts of breathsmoke out of a bluejay's mouth, the sign of the sound
of him standing on the feeder to make his own annunciation to the earth

he's the present epicentre of, and to me halted on its rim, hardly breathing.

A Few Facts

The chiming clock. The girl at her desk sneezing.
The hiss of traffic after rain has sleeked the street.
The chime sounding off the silent library air.
Outside, a kind of monumental after-icy-rain
relenting, something loosening and the ground
going soft, glistening, the water on it taking in
the world, the broad sycamore drawing water
up its roots, the huge trunk sopping it. In the room
the vase of Cremone daisies: yellow, white
and flaming orange. Shoes and books, a lit figure
bent to her work, lifting her shoulders slowly
up and looking out, letting a breath go. Smiling
when the child comes in with a question. Outside,
the spreading yellow maple shedding branches. A cairn
of bulky logs. Birds from dawn to dusk at the feeder:
black flashings across the blank window. The cats
dazzled, feeling the old hunger. Now the child
is posing, an arabesque, by the stove; now she's
wrapped in a rug, reading; now she is sitting up
in bed, a duchess, asking for her cardigan, grinning
at the laden tray—its porridge, milk, tea, striped napkin
in its ring—at light seeping through blue curtains.

Looking for a Book on Chardin

In the silence of the library, the hush
of its almost abstract emptiness
before it's full of buzzing students,

I'm searching for something, anything
that would tell me how the death
of his wife and the unspeakable death

of his two young daughters and the sad
end of his painter son under the murk
of canal water lapping at the Rialto

came home to the small stone altars
set in shades of grey paint on those
blank canvases Chardin livened

with dead animals and birds, their soft
fur and feather bodies stopped
in the still embrace of death, hung up

or laid out before our eyes in such silence
as denies nothing, finds no meanings,
only the facts themselves growing

clearer, sinking in this common quiet
as we take their careful measure
and step back to, more surely, see them.

Another Country

(Indoors Out)

Here is the country of doors and windows. Here is the house where the kitchen ghost mixes a marinade—*salt, mustard, ginger, pepper*—so your sister is still skipping rope in the front garden, waiting her turn to enter that charmed circle, her whole body bobbing, the rope thwacking concrete, the privet hedge not yet grown higher than the railings. And here is the bed where the bedroom phantom will ease as far into flesh as flesh can take, waiting for a pulse to answer, though no soul can hold it. Nobody did anybody any wrong, right? Yet smoke grows thicker, choking room after remembered room. And who's that weeping behind locked doors? And what are these body-shaped blocks of ice doing—kissing like that, glowing turquoise, as if metal had bled into heads melting together? And no way in the world to part them. Trampled to a rumpled crust of ice, the snow takes no tracks any more: nothing will leave even the lightest print, so you'll go invisible, or almost.

(Seaside)

Try the Bettystown smell of sand and dune grass because (infant in loving memory) you were born to it. Pram, sunshine, cottage forecourt, sky of green leaves. Gleam-heads of black knapweed. Purple loosestrife. Vanilla crests of meadow-sweet. All the live sparks montbretia starts. Glimmer-ditches. Say a small prayer now to Santa Botanica, patron of forget-me-nots and other painful cases. Hold on. Fidelity to skeletons is the missing link. Find it and everything will come clear—*as day,* I was about to say, but will you just look out this window: even our green hill's been smothered; lakeshine only a milky glitter. But see that small opening half-way up the ash tree? Where the wren entered? A cracked window, it is, of opportunity. Now see me. Vanish into it.

(Wardrobe)

Heart-constriction at the thought of that door from the kitchen out to the back garden, or that window letting in western light with its parade of spires, roof-slates, chimney-pots. Or the way their wardrobe was filled with promise or some darker invitation: go in, close the door, vanish into the time before you were at all, breathing its odours of mothball and lavender, feeling the thick-silky fox-head of fur, knowing the unfrocked mothersmell of dresses, how they swayed; the thin click of hangers; fatherscent of laundered shirts; the crisp fingertip feel of linen. All theirs, all there, and you might disappear into their pre-history, before you'd arrived, eyes and voices you'd never seen or heard. And never again such browns. Even the tall armoire in the room your lover lodged in wasn't it, its solid mahogany drawing to itself the lustrous rubbings of dusk—being an enigma impenetrable, imperturbable, no key in the lock. While the wardrobe in your parents' room was an open book, its pages adrift in infinity, woodshades, dark of the world.

What Matter

Does it matter, moon at full, that moonshine
comes streaming through the bedroom window—
a shower of mercury, luminous
in the early hours so the cats are wide-eyed
with anticipation, fretful at every whisper,
and we lie awake, counterpaned with light,
our thoughts free range, not to be tethered?

And does it matter that light, late afternoon,
makes every willow leaf, every mallard feather,
each bristling filament in the doe's freckled ear
show itself for what it is—a strand of *gold*
to airy thinness beat, a sort of spirit-tip to tug
us out of the big picture, put us in touch
with the far edge of things where the heart

has been in hiding, harking after what's taken
root there, distinct as dark-night starlight
but nameless, simply a glimmer of inscrutable
integrity, a way of standing to attention
for a second, tantalizing the eyes out of your head
with hope, till the opening closes over
and your eyes and all they fall on

are only blunt, colorless stone? Day after day
does it matter that the heart of the matter
in the heart's heavy, loving tussle
with what matters—to eye, ear, finger-ends,
to all the tidal turbulence of the senses—
may rest in, may indeed come down to, this
momentary unfolding to blind spots, blankness?

Discovery

The hare, they say, is very fragile, but when I saw one
crisscross the boggy lakeshore pasture, another
flick its shape like a brown shadow between hedges
while another stood on long hind legs and sniffed
the still air in which nothing moved but its own
weird ears as another huddled in the ragged shadow
of a clump of rushes and waited till its mate
was huddled beside it, then dashed a zigzag
and was followed—both vanishing into furze—then

I had to believe they were beyond fragility, creatures
so close to earth they'd taken of its strength and could
conjure with it, and I envied them their agility, their
lightness of touch, such instinctive cut and dash
to safety of a sort, that quick companionable coupling
in spite of the riotous babble-jabber of nerves
or the flaring eye, the frantic leap. To be always on the run
ahead of the hunt, with some spot always in an almost
invisible country to home to, drawing breath together.

Something

Something to do with how raindazzle at cloudbreak
touches up three apples in their skins and makes them blush
teal, cinnabar, gamboge; something with how that swan

stands splayed, a lovely alien, on slime-covered stones
at Claddagh-mouth; the cormorant speeding downstream
has something to do with it, taking advantage of the Corrib's

last mad dash for the sea, scattering black-headed, crack-
voiced gulls, keen gliders, eyes like needles in their search
for scraps, casual vigilantes of anything out of the ordinary

run of things on the river; and something about how
those clouds pack their massy granite granaries with light—
makes me ask what law in physics keeps these bottles

and bits of chipped wood in the turbulent trough
of the small waterfall spinning and spiraling, fleeing
in circles, going nowhere: however far they fling

themselves in the roil and roaring foamburst, they're
caught and drawn in, at once fugitive and centripetal,
stuck where they are while something in them seems

a big breathless thrusting out that won't give up
the struggle, though it avails nothing, simply brings all
back where it began, dizzy with longing, starting over

again, and again over again, as if it meant something.

In Bits

Living as we do
in a *constellation of patches,*
there's always something

to be said for the partial
and imperfect, all the unfinished
bits and pieces that keep

catching hold of odd angles
of light, little unstitched strips
of unexpected colour (say

celery, bone, lava, cornflower,
lemon-juice) clotting on
car bonnets or asleep all day

in mud puddles or negotiating
with the barrels of big guns
aimed from the badger-grey

deck of a destroyer due east
while you're watching
how a small ginger-winged thing

with legs and gold antennae
atop the tip of a concrete
corner of wall the late

October sun's rebounding off
just stands there as something
happens to its eyes

and to the brazen chain-mail
of its dorsal plate, happens
in scraps—something that keeps

edging out of the desirous
reach of speech: tiny knives
of light, off-key neural music

finding the proper pitch
for jigging hither and yon
along the length and breadth

of one entirety: being it.

Signland

Cicadas tear the air to flitters.
Stitch it together again
as though nothing had happened.

All the leaves of the locust trees
have been leached of greenness, burned
the brown of a penitential habit:
Brother Fungus does it.

Spectral mushrooms
bulging out of leaf mulch:
here, believe me,
the resurrection of the dead.

And what is that phantom raccoon doing,
staring us down by daylight—
little black-mask sadly lolling?

The signs are not propitious,
though locked
two by two in turquoise glimmerflight
the dragon- and damsel-flies

rise and fall,
thrusting and trusting each other
over water

where the lone heron stands
reading his own face, patient
as daylight and waiting
in a long day's silence

for another life to happen
suddenly upon it
and be the sense at last—

sweet-pulsing, full-blooded, bright
and beyond question—
he was hoping for.

Weather Channel

Midwinter

As the hawk—come to wary rest at the top of the pine tree and hasped to a bare branch there—is harried by crow after crow making black swooping attacks, so my head sits staring out at a world encased in cold. In the maple, in the Scots pine, in the dead of winter, two squirrels are building nests of dead leaves—flimsiest defense against the coming chill, the snow their noses and bones keep telling them is on its way: its dark wing will unfurl first, then close, then open, shedding its load of blinding cold that slow-gathers into a white silence in which my daughter will walk about without me, whistling to herself her secret song and remembering how we'd walk and talk—catching the crisp crunch of our footsteps over snow and ice-packed earth, straying between subjects, listening to each other.

May Day

Everything flushed, fattening to overload. Pinks, greens, whites gleaming towards the somnolent luxury of their own abundant coming. Blossoms, leaves, catkins and other dangle-pods. Air a golden lung swollen with pollen. Grass covered suddenly with bodies in heat, baring themselves to the hip: arms glistering, legs scissoring, naked soles drumming greensward: young men and women letting the blood run into each scented instant of *be all, end all.* Maybe it's the only way. In the old days, it was all—youth, age, life *in extremis*—all abstract: a pan-shot of surf striking, its slow motion unfolding towards creamy manes, a flared transparency of wings in which light hung transfixed, a visionary wholeness you almost began to believe in. Not this actual awful close-up force and uproar.

Turtle and Two Girls

Sunglossed blunt head of a turtle over water.
My two daughters stand at the grassy verge
and wonder: size, age, power of the creature
at ease in the middle of its world and breathing
the same lush early autumnal air as they do
with their tall bodies, pale legs, rapt faces.

Keeping their gaze fixed on that sleek head,
they wait its next move, which is simply
to sink into one of its elements—native as it is
to earth and water, ambivalently at home
in flickering weed-green depths or among dry leaves
of grass—the way a mystery may show itself,

then sink from sight, dreamlike, disappearing
into the dizzy whirl we have to live in
as these two girls have to turn back now to what
they were at before this swimmer into their ken
connected—one jogging home, the other sitting
to get lost again in the book she was reading.

Simple Pleasures

How even a simple mantra *(carrots, ginger, scallions, mint)*
can make my mouth water, nose itch with a sudden flux
of appetite, a little tongue-lust for these aromas rising
like the dead at the resurrection of the body—perfect
and *permeable,* bright body-shades drifting into
the next phase, trailing glory-clouds and taking a last look

at the solid stuff they're leaving: grass, edible roots, leaves,
the spectral fluctuations sunset paints over the lower sky,
how jut of cliff and spinal ridge-work resolve the outline
of mountains, all the unknown familiar five o'clock
downtown faces. As how, in bed this morning, the line
from shoulder to nipple signified wholeness, integrity and—

with my hand on it, under the tracing weight of my eye—
simple pleasure. Or how, at noon off the beaten track,
sitting in a shaded weed patch to picnic, we're happy
in a hot silence broken by breeze-gusts shaking down
in loud whispers the leaves. Briared about, up to its stuck
wheels in rust and poison ivy, an ancient farm machine

defies us to identify its bars, rods, shafts, gear-cogs
and bent axles, all at terminal rest in a nest of silence. Once
it was a clatter of joyous noise—ploughing or harrowing
or making hay, air braced by a dream of harvest. Now
it shimmers like ore or the weathered bones of an old
horse, a wreath of sumac leaves gleaming between them.

Exhibition

Morning muddy blue. Beyond the Hudson a shadow of green
says grass. Up early, I saw a starling with straw in its beak
staring about, eager-eyed for a site—starting from scratch
its safe household, branching out, a body of flit and twitter, truly
looking. And now I'm trying to see what prickle-leafed flower

Vermeer's spaniel is eyeing beside Diana's bare feet and that
brimming paten of bright gold, its bronze-umber water. And look
there, behind glass, glaring out at all gawkers, the panther
soul, explosive, of Carel Fabritius. Avert. Walk on. Proceed
to see pearl earrings, and a chair Johannes gave Pierre

who found good use for it. And here is the white mare
Paulus Potter left, standing wise-eyed in an archway of light
from nowhere, gazing through that wide-open barn door
into God knows what future, the face of her furrowed master
mildly blazing. But how will we find our way

out of this little street? The house a rose-bricked, mullion-windowed,
olivegreen-and-wine-shuttered casket of darkness; a woman—
white-bonneted—bent forever over her sewing in the doorway
where the light is right. I wonder if, starting from such courtyards,
the meek will really inherit earth, even what they know of it:

maybe no more than the warm weight of a small dog asleep
on the child's lap in a corner of infinity—where the heart
of light is beating, wing-like, seeking a spot to rest itself
among our everyday tables, folds of cloth, kitchen utensils,
and where this other woman, with her hand out in a dazed

hover-haze of her own, is opening or about to close the window.

Ladybird and Mother

Sunday air thronged to throttling with ladybirds
opening and closing their wings, tiny gold buttons
that click and zip and glisten in the gold of October
and land on any leaf or level stretch of grass
or hot brick simmering in the glare. You used to see them
one at a time, and there'd be a minute's rapture
over the blessing of good luck: you'd make a wish
and watch the diminutive creature stretch its wings
and lift off the kitchen windowsill and vanish
into the branches of our neighbour's apple tree.
But why this black-freckled red or yellow beetle
conveyed good fortune, your guess was as good as mine,
though we knew it was under *Our Lady's* protection,
one more leftover from the age of faith you still
lived in—its garden appetites (gobbling aphids)
making this six-legged carapace a seasonal benediction,
as it still is for farmers: a sign of health in green leaf
and blossom, auguring a fine spring, no one
wanting to bring down out of the innocent blue
the bad luck in killing one, cleaving the clear line
of connection spreading from all corners of that
coleopterous cradle-world to the two of us
crunching into a ripe pippin. It was our kind
of superstition: small enough to fit in a kitchen garden
and not needing—as scarab or scorpion needs—
the sands of Egypt or vasty veldts of Africa
to dazzle in. This very minute *(the luck of it!)* my west-
facing window has a dozen contemplative ladybirds
flickering in their Sabbath trance on it. And listen:
Come back, they're whispering, *and wish on us.*

Going Gone

It's the way things rush away from us into the shade
of our unknowing, into the thickness of time gone by

and felt like a chunk of dusk squatting in the room
with you, airless and immovable, darkly, terminally

blank—a silent, faceless thing slumped in the corner.
This morning I caught at a small distance the fleet

shapes of two deer running among the stark uprights
of trees—*deer-tree-deer-tree-tree-deer*—flickering away

in fright, giving me this heady mix of the quick
and the still: stuttering light-shapes between the trees,

legs bending and straightening, bodies flexing into
each final formulation, tails gleaming white as the snow

they were bounding over, where I found their clean
prints: cloven ideograms for *cold-open-field-fright,*

small hammers designed for some unusual task, two
fat teardrops salting their own strict figure in snow.

A going, I mean, that leaves little (but that little
a burning) after it, as five high sky-ducks, for example,

leave a vacant space of blaze in their wake, that cross
a gem-like sky, flashquacking at the sound barrier.

Rome, the Pantheon

Under this perfect circle of light that is the sky
roofing the centre-space of the Pantheon, once
I stood with my father, looking up and listening
to his wonder—no common moment for that
man of sober nerve, sense of dread, on edge
until an early beer would settle him. But there

we were for once, at the centre of the house
of all the gods and *(imagine!)* marveling together,
where now on a shaft of sunlight a butterfly
becomes a fluttering double wing of white fire,
a bit of angelbody made flesh or nearly flesh
for us for an accidental minute, to be a brief

blaze in our dimension, then rise up through
that true skylight and keep on going back—
back into its own invisible realm where stone
and circle, flesh and family are translated
into simple light, a single lifetime burning
one big instant and becoming *(look!)* infinity.

On Change

What, if not transformation, is your urgent command?
RILKE

(Body Language)
It comes close to *plenitude,* filling the moment as the moment becomes smoke, then smell, the odour of apple pulp up and down the Hudson Valley, whole orchards crushed and milled into cloudy cider, its colour the tint that leaves turn when they shake themselves free of rain that settled all night upon them to the noise of thunder, the deluge decanted out of the dark, bending branches till day came back, its light and heat unloading that wet weight, the tempest trundling westward over the Catskills so leaves, lightened, dry a few more shades away from green toward the many-mansioned father-house of brown. A scent between sweet and tart, the homegrown satisfactions of its earthen flavours filling every corner of the mouth and mind, drawing us back as if we'd never abandoned or been cast out of that first garden with its *continual spring, and autumn there continual,* the air all auburn, peach, bronze and polished pewter, its silken touches tendering our cheeks and hands, the smell of apples offering their mottled skin and cool white flesh to us, the senses blessed by this seasoned spirit as, drop by drop, it oozes into us.

(From the Train)
If you move fast enough, how nearly abstract everything appears—even the lordly horizontal of the Hudson and the hills hoisting up blue-misty from the far shore as pyramids and black rectangles; even this grid of reeds, its tawny cage pasted to my moving window. Sky only a canvas with all the white and blue drawn out of it, an immensity no name will anchor. Otherwise all is ripple or glitter, is flat or ruffled, roughed up to this anonymous shade—that isn't grey, or white, but like light itself turned to a scrim of dust; but not that either, rather a kind of crystallized transparency, a waxed, bare, see-through substance, mere nakedness

made visible—on which the iron glyph for *bridge* is stenciled, small shapes adrift along it. So living bits and pieces, figures of *things,* inhabit the flatness of abstraction until, slowed down, you start to see them for birds—not just *birdshapes* but gulls flapping calmly downstream—or for the solid rusted stark remains of warehouse sheds, embankment buildings, wormy dark up-juts of old wood pilings, or that tall orphaned factory chimney, all (as you slow towards Harlem) come back to claim their proper particular life, returning the world. So abstraction, which takes up—beyond our everyday touch and go—its fixed abode at the fast heart of things, diminishes, and is hidden.

Cézanne and Family

When he was excavating form from facts—
finding the geometry of trees and Mont Sainte Victoire—
he was doing what I'd like to find
a byway to, translating ravages of daily dross

into an illuminated shape or two, simple as light
but holding all the prickly specific unspeakable
matter of fact, a *grasping-at* (think the thousand
cuts of colour, paint laid and layered, angling

into a new veracity), that offers a centre
but no easy symmetry, coming to a point, yes,
but letting the disorderly goings-on of nature
go on, undisciplined as they are

and no containing them. Could it be like families,
I wonder, the way they don't or rarely ever
make clear and formal sense and yet the facts
add up and we stand there, astonished by them?

Bee Fuchsia

At the first brief lull
in terrible weather
bees are back, each
entering headfirst
the upside-down open
nectar-heavy skirts
of wet fuchsia flowers
and seeming to stay
quite still in that laden
inner space, only
the smallest shudder
of the two together
when the bee-tongue
unrolls and runs
its tiny red carpet
into the heart
of what is no mystery
but the very vanishing
point and live centre
of the flower's instant
irrevocable unfolding,
then stillness again
while this exchange
(layer after layer of
dusty goodness lipped,
given) is taking place—
the flower flushed
and swelling a little,
the bee gently but
hungrily clutching.

III

Edge

When I walked out to the sea surfing and spuming
into meerschaum heaps of lettuce-tinted gauze—
breakers becoming light, then noise, the ocean raging
and rearranging this long spit of sand like a life
at the mercy of circumstance—and saw the north wind

drive trillions of sandgrains to scour every last trace
of what the previous tide had done, and gulls snatch
huge clamshells from the swirl and smash them
to get at and gobble each salt, soft-bodied helplessness
at the heart of its own broken home, then I felt caught

between water-violence and the gulls' patience,
between the shifting ground I stood on and the thunder-
turbulence of water, between a slowly disappearing
ceiling of cloud and the blue sky-cupola it leaves
behind. Between titanic ocean-roar and ticking heart

was the brink I stood on, taking stock of what lived
between me and that razor's edge where the horizon
laid a seam so sky and sea could greet each other:
those panic-depths of pursuit and capture; the mad
harrow-squirm of teeming life; blind appetite in action.

The Next Parish

If we could feel in the day by day
the way things are—as Pissarro
saw the road to Gisors in winter
and the town of Pontoise
opening its homespun serge and ochre
heart to him, its footpaths and roof-tiles
clotted with snow, the vegetable seller's
big-wheeled barrow
clattering on cobbles; if we could feel
as he did the extension of that
into the next parish, where love
clear-eyed and unhurried
keeps house—a space
uncluttered yet accommodating
everything in and out
of the ordinary, shying away
from nothing; if this could be
how our bodies got beyond
the habit-ridden, time-throttled
tenements of rose and ice,
it might be possible to pierce
the mist of things rose-tinted
and conjure from that tattered sleeve
some sign
that the way, though strait,
was passable, even in winter.

The Curve

First, the blunt integrity of the jet's engine: snub-nosed
and bursting with thrust-potential, ponderously perched
for take-off under a cloudy sky, murmuring and growling
to itself in its dialect of imperatives and unimpeachable
nouns, waiting for the word to go. Then the quick series
of sparked explosions out of sight, the wild takeover towards
the hands of chance, too fast for thought as you keep going

into the blur of possibility becoming what is as is, and soon—
rising on this inhuman burst of speed—the world spreads
under you its miniature concerns: houseblocks and toy cars,
the snow-white tablecloths and handkerchiefs of fields,
the child's map of spider-roads stippled with quill-trees,
the home ground shrinking to fit in the palm of your hand,
all creaturely concerns dimming and disappearing
like figures down the wrong end of a telescope. Then

it's cloudlife for a little while, the quick judder of sudden
turbulence to put your heart crosswise, till you're above
that too and in the clear. And you could be alone up there
with a world of wonders under you, going on as if
it were all in your will, you intended it, and there's time
to see earth be simple landscape, salvaged from its
own ungainly details by the saving grace of elevation,
the small unspoken hope it offers, till you're descending

again, entering the cloud again and lost in it, waiting—
while your heart is all eyes winkling the mist—
for a sign, the whole thing that holds you holding steady

in ways you can't begin to fathom, until your fond desire
becomes a kind of Orpheus in the overworld, a force
of fixed attention bringing things to bear until at last
you're through, the green ground again rising to greet you.

Smoke

Out of the blue. Out of the blue sky. Out of the blue sky over Manhattan. Out of the blue. Steelsmoke. Glasssmoke. Cloudsmoke. Bodysmoke. Screamsmoke over the roar. Blacksmoke. Black. Quick as thought the news traveling. Gone. Guns in the air. *Murdered sleep*. In the sunshine. A helicopter heading south. Its shadow-wings and shadow-blades slicing buildings, blacking our standing figures looking up. The quick of it passing into the blue. Wait for it wait for it wait for it: the names, pillars of smoke, broken altar, silence. Reel of names. No one not there. Dirty joke of a laugh. The news not yet. Maybe it will not have happened. Bee shadow over the open page: *blank, shadow, blank*. Sounds from the street: the traffic beginning again as it must. Turn the page, another, another. Allblank. From their camps and bunkers they watch. The big men in uniforms and suits are watching and the small masked men in waiting are watching. Smoke. Cloudroar of smoke on the screen. Rewind. Roll it again. Again.

Then

Afterword (The Teacher Thinks about His Students)

All they want is adequate speech. So we reach across the Great Plains of the classroom table, tripping over our words. It will never be enough. Eyes of the lost. Tears where one is looking at me, trying to speak. *What man, ne'er pull your hat about your brows.* When I draw down the blinds, a sky of rubble and smoke is swept away to nothing, a blank. I know this script. It beggars translation. *Dispute it like a man?* Syllable by syllable the story *(story!)* is coming out—of red headbands, box-cutters, plastic knives. A book (a *book!*) of simple instructions. Barking and barked, lovingly, yes, at one another. First this, then that, then the other, and we are *(praise Heaven!)* home. Poor eyes drowning and no one to ask. *Please is my name on your list it is my father no is there another list?* When the book is passed from hand to hand to hand it falls open at "Smoke." It hurts to squint through it. A grievous affliction. To imagine we might loosen our tongues. That we might go on. They've gone home now, hungry as field-mice in February. In silence. Not one crumb of comfort among them.

Afterimage (From the New Jersey Turnpike)

Through the washed blue mist of heat the city's a shadow-city traced on rice-paper, a gauze gleam over the blue sheen of water. It is that kind of morning, no mourning for a minute at least, until—behind the chalky scrim of things seen at a distance (a set of floating forms sketching *Manhattan*)—the shape of what's missing makes its presence felt and my eyes are all over the place, not finding. But the morning is still a feast for sight, and in words like *North* and *South,* and in that truck I haven't looked for in the mirror, I recover the way of our world again—its crushed animals, burnt-out cars, the silence of solitude while moving at high speed, the beautiful lost faces of the drivers as they disappear into the distant conflagration of trees, the shadow a line of geese draws along the horseshoe of a stone bridge in sunshine. And, where borders stiffen between states, this hail of radiance I'm rushing into.

And So On

Stained-glass blue day. But smoke, after a noise
to deafen, still drifts half a world away
over fallen houses. Soot-faced, the winged boys

turn for home, the word *mission* still warm,
still pungent in the mouth. Little wonder the sky
when you lift your splitting head to its glare

is heavy with questions, though earth here
is harrowed and seeded: sleek leaves, grass-blades
barely showing—just enough to say *green*

in the blazing face of heaven. But now—
the spongy simmer of autumn still bubbling—
how can these migrant juncos have come

to our berried hedges and overhanging canopies
of leaf, their voices silver-tinkling mini-bells
of glass? And how can a few human voices

hope to hold the blood to all it promises, all
the market-place chaos of colour and tongues
and the whole thing *working*? Simple wishes

for a post-war world of touch in earnest,
when—smoke cleared, cries died down—snow
covers the only ground left to stand on.

Drained Lake, Heron in Mud

When I saw the heron standing up to its spindleshins in mud
where the lake's deep water only yesterday caught the light
and cracked it into a scatter of small flames, each fragment
of fractured mirror grasping a colour-shard of sky or leaf
or the glancing glimpse of a wing flapping over (taupe
for goose, grey and blue a jay, diverse shades of white
the gulls), when I saw that statued bird, light burning its beak
to an aluminum triangle, a tapered hammerhead of glass,
it could have been the sign I was searching for: a solitary creature

dealing with this unsettled set of fresh conditions, not stuck
in the mud but surrounded by it, trying to draw something
to live by from it, some surprise live morsel that would make
survival possible. So I walked the bank and looked at it
from every angle, hoping to pick a hint or two might help
shed any ray of light on things. But it just stood hunched,
ruffling once, twice, its shoulder feathers, the gleam of its beak
flashing back unreadable semaphore. I imagined its keen eyes'
amber, their stapled gaze. And that it was not at ease, but patient.

Harmonia

The shape a solitary oarsman makes as he dips and lifts his two blades
and they pend a second or two like thin wings angled from the scull
and leave behind him on the blue skin of water the clean design
of a fish—spine and ribs exactly finished where the sunstruck Schuylkill

sickles Philadelphia. How the precise line of hills west of the Hudson
is etched by the sun gone behind them, and the air's incarnadined—
as a fire might start inside your skin and flush your bones to visibility,
making your shape more absolute, bright, and final than I can imagine.

Or how a dancer I know moves across campus this mist-shawled morning,
her book-satchel swaying off one shoulder and her black clogs glistening
with wet grass, a green sweater bunched at her waist—letting me see
how a body can be at one with itself, every part moving together, lifting her

above the clutch of gravity the way a rising flock of starlings opens, closes
so it might be one body, but *distributed,* feeling bound like that and free.

Fix

Spread of light: momentary
molecular bristle of it
over your skin: how it
scrambles matter, so we need
painters (Caravaggio, say)

to slow it down, come
to rest in things, helping them
grow single, distinct
in a blaze of shade—every thread
a mote amazed at being intact

and turning its back
on change. Otherwise
we're only passing through—
a bruised leg curving
from light to dark; a blur

of flesh against the blond
wood of a doorframe—
only the helpless exposure
of things in spacetime
if the painter's eye and hand

fail to fix them. *Fix* them,
meaning make them
as they are, meaning *Look,*
we're here too: a burst fig;
the harp shape, heat-glazed,

of a cricket; the sorrowful
sympathy in the ram's eye
as he offers himself
next in line to the knife—
a creamy blue sky brightening

that lambent, mild iris.

Goldcrest

You lift your eyes from Hopkins' hard grief—
how he's desperate for some smile behind
cloud and mountain, any wisp of respite
would let him have pity on his poor Jackself,
see daylight beyond the blinding dark
he's groped about for his soul in—lift them
to the tiny bird feeding from leaves, so
alive in the one moment of its unfolding
it flings you into a life so concentrated
it makes its own halo, nothing but
instant after instant of appetite its abiding.

for the minute of your distraction
nothing matters but this quick-eyed glint
of single-minded hunger among sally leaves
in shadow, grey-greens tilting silver
when the breeze flex-fumbles among them
to conceal the bird, tawny wings camouflaged
by leaf-flutter, that composes a whole life
out of its few desires (to survive, to stay
like Hopkins alive to the slightest shift
in currents of air, the colour in *pearly shadows*
or clouds lead-tinged and *ruddled*), no gap

between seeing what's wanted
and springing to it, as if the raddled angst
you've spent the morning picking at is nothing
but sudden steel and silver manifestations of rain
which this nimble killer of spiders and woodlice
knows will give way to other weathers,
the shine and shade of things impossible

to lay a restraining hand on, the way
(molten gold-bead on its brow) it goes
about its own business, its brazen engagement
with each famishing, ravishing, riven
nano-second—then goes, no stopping it.

Photo of Matisse

Clutching a dove in his fist
he looks at it like an open book,
reading the bird's black eyes
that startle back astonished

at the fierce eye-balling attention
leveled at it—one creature
staring another down. He peers
with that impersonal intensity

any painter aims at his subject—
a curiosity fixed and calm
as that of astronomer or pathologist
mapping a planet, naming a wound.

The bird, I imagine, believes
it's about to be eaten, and would
with its own infinite curiosity
look its end in the eye, becoming it.

Silence. A matter after all
of life and death. A poise
perfected; a third thing made:
to be looked at, looking back.

Beholding the Hare

In the gale that's trying to take the roof off this small house,
shaking it to its rocky foundations, the hare is making
his rounds of the garden. Wet morning light shows me
ears hemmed in white, their black points, how they flatten
when the wind roars, rise and swivel when he hunkers under
the shelter of hedges or against the drenched stones of the wall.

All he knows is the way the weather is, how it wraps him
in its fits and starts, a sort of swirling whirligod whose breath
he must, turn and turn about, huddle from or bask in. Now
he stretches to get at a darkgreen left-over bramble leaf, all else
bare as sea-beaten stone and showing to the wind and rain
its skin, its bone—tree-bark bright as those blackcurrant eyes

that read the world like a book, each page changing the story
no matter what we or the hare or that one ruffled chaffinch
balancing between red and yellow pegs on the clothesline
can make of it. Right now, what strikes me is the hare's
star-sharp singularity, how he's all of a piece, each particle
wholly in the present moment, from the ink-tip of an ear

to the chalk-tuft under his raised tail, from the fur-coated ripple
that's all muscle when he tenses a haunch, to the delicate tremor
his nose makes as it fetches the rest of the world into the realm
of his understanding, that many-scented evanescence in the wind
of things, what his eye can't find, nor his tongue touch,
nor the soft fingers of his fur make sense of, nor his quick ears

swiveling to every whisper—but which the snub, brown
shiver-button of his nose finds, filling out his feeling
for the world, any minute of which would take me an age

of translation to carry over even a hint of, knowing no words
for his wholeness, for all the stuff of sense registering at once
on the shell of him, how he's the kernel of its kinetic wheeling

by just being there, free of memory and forecast, being at one
with possibility like that, and not at odds, not split in the middle
and out of focus, not feeling the very ground nerved and veined
with *tremor cordis,* fault lines branching every which way
from the lost centre, the heart itself out of tune, unable to contain
itself. Not, that is, one of us: soul-searching in our skin of reason.

A Thrush by Utamaro

Although it looks the picture of perfect balance, and although I'd imagined nothing could be steadier (yellow legs locked fast to the softer yellow of a bamboo stake), and envied its way—at once solid and light—of being in the world, in fact the bird only appears in the painting for its name, *komadori,* which means *to be unbearably troubled.* But then I see that what I was really admiring is the way its tenacious grip on things is sustained in spite of how the world of broken stake and bursting chrysanthemum blossom is going to bits around it, its unbearable trouble being borne and lived inside as the creature must live inside its own name, remaining upright against the odds and holding on to that long bamboo as though it were a flute, whose music might match the thrush's own woodnotes, songs raised over wreckage when the dust has settled.

What Happened

When out of the choppy, colloped water at bankside,
out of the dark of the pond's broken mirror,
out of the early morning air lit at intervals
to ginger and claret and fading amber

a heron unfolded and floated away, barely grazing
wind-crinkled water to land on the far shore
and fold itself over itself again and vanish
into the grey ground over there, it was surprise

enough, I thought, to carry me through
to the end of my walk. But then the skunk
in its humped lumbering scuttle crossed my path,
its back an acetylene gleam, its head invisible as it

hurries into a dried-out stand of chokecherry canes
where it lodges itself under a rustling
quilt of dead leaves, lying low
till the sound of my steps will have receded

and left this morning world of ours
be a silent wide untroubled space
for it to find its winding, quiet way through,
its path home marked by signs

we could make no sense of, stuck, as mostly we are,
inside the spindle-cell of our hidebound five senses
stumped and blunted by being too long
in the cushioned grip of ease to be unscripted,

though once or twice you might find
wild words in your mouth, know
their barbed dark speed and lethal illumination—
the way any unhoused creature will strike

and snarl and settle for no less than the gesture
that will be its saving grace, surprising itself
by being suddenly all there, knowing its moment,
as I knew the moment when I saw the heron first

and then the white glide of the skunk across my path
that I was *there,* that *meeting* had materialized, was
passing from the moment but had been there
in the *here-now* beyond question, in which

the instant burned to life, then ash. Had happened.

Steady Now

Although things vanish, are what mark our vanishing,
we still hold onto them—ballast against the updraft
of oblivion—as I hold onto this umbrella in a world of rain,

of heavy wet greens and greys dissolving into a new
atmosphere, an underwater dulled electric glow
off everything, the air itself drowning in it, breath

thickening, growing mould. Yesterday I felt the smell
of grass greeting me as across a great distance, trying
to tell me one good thing in an underglaze of memory,

some forgotten summer trying to speak its piece. It is
the way of things and it never stops, never calls a halt—
this knocking and dismantling, this uprooting, cutting out

and digging down, so tall oaks and honey locusts
are laid low and drop to earth like felled cattle, shaking
the ground we've taken a stand on as if it were a steady

establishment, a rock of ages to outface ruin itself, not
the provisional slippery dissolving dissolute thing it is—
which we have against all the evidence set our hearts on.

Wildflowers in a Glass of Water

(Signorelli, *Pala di Sant' Onofrio*)

Cross-legged, a child angel
sits on the bottom step
of the throne of the merciful
Madonna and her human child.

Flanked by four saints—
rapt in their own sphere
of sanctity and paint—the angel
tunes his lute, holding its belly

close to his own plump
drum of a belly. Next
to his bare angelic foot
stands a glass of water

in which (drooping a little
but still alive) lean
three wildflowers
with exuberant petals and pale

exactly modeled stems: one
a dark March violet, the others
pink campion, their bladders
deftly rendered, so we may see

that in this grand, sanctified zone
where the infant god
shoulders his lily
like a pike or a white rifle

the painter had time
and knew the world had space
for these light morsels
of the ordinary, these

atoms of the everyday
to hold their own
and anchor us, gracing
the big picture.

Intermission

They're feeding each other, two small birds
swiveling on a sea-stone, open beaks
kissing and closing—creatures seeing to
each other's needs without question, drawing
the big world into their brief circle
of wing-quiver, heart-shiver, quick cries
as if the nerves themselves gave tongue,
the path between desire and satisfaction
shorter than thought, the ground dividing
being from being—one flesh-protected
spark of life from another—covered
in no time, so even time, for the moment,
is a matter of no moment, smoke that's
melted into air, into thin air, to leave
but a flaring thing behind: candescent
and burning its brief interval till all is ash,
redemptive breath recovering itself,
eyes seeking in eyes an answer
to what's happened. The fire at the heart
of things is what these two birds ignite
in their give and take, saying we live
in the one world—where some law
of loving exchange is, too, what tends the blaze
and can startle us into a kind of intermission
of peace between two clamorous cliff-
crumbling waves that rear, break, roar
and rip to shreds a coast of stone, unsettling
the air we stand in with a surf-storm
of salt-light that bites our eyes, blinding them.

Opposing Forces

Even in this sharp weather there are lovers everywhere
holding onto each other, hands in one another's pockets
for warmth, for the sense of *I'm yours,* the tender claim
it keeps making—one couple stopping in the chill
to stand there, faces pressed together, arms around
jacketed shoulders so I can see bare hands grapple
with padding, see the rosy redness of cold fingers
as they shift a little, trying to register through fold
after fold, *This is my flesh feeling you you're feeling.*

It must be some contrary instinct in the blood
that sets itself against the weather like this, brings
lovers out like early buds, like the silver-grey catkins
I saw this morning polished to brightness
by ice overnight. Geese, too: more and more couples
voyaging north, great high-spirited congregations
taking the freezing air in and letting it out
as song, as if this frigid enterprise were all joy,
nothing to be afraid of.

Workman

He stands, first, on a mechanical platform, higher than this high window. At his own level, fenced-in, he leans to dab dashes of mortar at a crenellated granite angle of the library tower. Stepping on the border rail, he swings one leg over the fence to get at a tricky inch and balances there: flicking mortar, smoothing and pointing, the strap stretched to its limit, holding him. Legs braced against metal, his left hand dips, takes, leans, spreads, points. His white hard-hat gleams. Simply a thick shadow on the blue canvas of a clear November sky, he seems relaxed as anyone on *terra firma,* though only scraps of steel and a leather belt prevent him plummeting. Entirely focused, he gets on with the job, and I feel my heart clenching, unclenching, just to see his shade making shapes on the stone: how he might be dancing.

(13.xi. 01)

The Search

It's the sheer tenacity of the clematis clinging to
rusty wire and chipped wood-fence that puts this
sky-blue flare and purple fire in its petals. To be
new in autumn, in mid-September, to be showing
yourself like that, naked as water under full moonlight:

something has to be good in such a world, in the talent
it has for lasting and coming back, in the way
it decorates our graves, our standing walls, our back
porches, and in the way the late bee lands
on its dazzle, walks the circumference of every petal

in some minor key of astonishment—drinking
the last of its sapphire wine. What takes shape
is a cellular sense of how the moment is jammed
to splitting with excess, each pod and sweet kernel
plumped to bursting with the brash simplicities

of contradiction, the child's tears watering the plant
that seems from a shrivel of bones to make itself
an azure conflagration, seeming to say, *There's
always more to say.* Language can be like that,
taking its stand on the driest, most barren space

of clay, asking only that we attend, behold it being
no more than being itself—*a Nothing /. . . blooming.*
And tonight the old man, your father, smiled twice:
once when he'd reached the sofa after the fifty-mile
shuffle from the hall door; once when his tongue

tasted the tart cool of a spoonful of blueberries
and he turned his eyes, shining their milky blue, on the child
who lifted her brimming spoon and smiled back at him.

(for Rachel)

Cold Comfort

Snow loosening its hair, letting it fall
in streams, snow that was knotted up
with cold . . .

The light dying and you look back at it. *Now,*
she said, *he is a god of glimmer,* meaning Apollo
or some other deity of desire and motion. Odd

that in the inexpressible inside, the tenanted void
of the center, you can recognize but put no name
to the way you are yourself, only feeling it

in the instant of its disappearing: smoke-bubbles
of breath on a cold morning. You are not
what you were, but between one blink and another

something in you knows how it was, knowing
Being for what it is, and is no more. My mother
would put it more simply: *To air,* is what she'd say,

throwing open a door, a window, folding back
bedclothes, or hanging blankets out in the garden
in the sun *to air,* so they could live the way

they were meant to. Now, when blood is fired
by the first true sunny day of spring, my students—
like birds feeling the migratory buzz

in their airy bones—shed their clothes like leaves
and flop themselves headlong down on the winter-
scarred remnants of grass, and adore their own

overgod, faces all eager to be lit and filled
by heat, riddled by light, while the last low
mound of snow dwindles minute by minute,

from which I scoop a handful and walk
with its chill reminder, squeezing snow to ice, ice
to freezing water, taking the last bit—big

as a plum but no plum-sweetness to it—
into my mouth, making my teeth ache as I
eat the end of winter, and swallow it down.

Out of reluctant matter
What can be gathered? Nothing, beauty at best.

CZESLAW MILOSZ, "No More"

Notes

The Celan epigraph is from *Selected Poems and Prose of Paul Celan,* translated by John Felstiner (W. W. Norton, 2001). That by Wallace Stevens is from *The Collected Poems of Wallace Stevens* (Vintage Books, 1990).

"Start of March, Connemara": The Elizabeth Bishop poem I implicitly allude to is "The End of March."

"Wing and Prayer": The first phrase in italics is a mix of a passage from *Hamlet* and a passage from Wordsworth's "Ode: Intimations of Immortality from Recollections of Early Childhood."

"Another Week with Hölderlin": The epigraph is from "The Rhine," and the italicized quotations in each of the days are from, respectively, "Greece," "Mnemosyne," "The Rhine," "The Migration," "The Only One," "Remembering," and "Patmos." The translations are by Richard Sieburth, in *Hymns and Fragments by Friedrich Hölderlin* (Princeton University Press, 1984).

"April Note": The phrase in italics is from *The Winter's Tale* (II. iii).

"Foam": the italicised words refer to concepts in contemporary physics. "The quantum vacuum is thought of as a seething froth of real particle/virtual particle pairs going in and out of existence continuously and very rapidly." (Lama Anagarika Govinda, *Foundations of Tibetan Mysticism,* 1969.)

"In Bits": The phrase in italics is from "July Mountain" by Wallace Stevens.

"On Change": The Rilke epigraph is from the Ninth "Duino Elegy," translated by Stephen Mitchell, in *The Selected Poetry of Rainer Maria Rilke* (Vintage Books, 1982).

"The Next Parish": The phrase in italics is from "Man and Bottle" by Wallace Stevens.

"Smoke" and "Then": Some passages in italics are from *Macbeth,* especially the scene (IV.iii) in which Macduff learns of the murder of his wife and children.

"Fix": The Caravaggio painting I have in mind at the end is *The Sacrifice of Isaac.*

"Goldcrest": Words in italics are taken from Gerard Manley Hopkins, *Poems and Prose* (Penguin, 1953).

"A Thrush by Utamaro" responds to an illustration in the 2001 desk calendar *(Art of Japan: A Celebration)* from the Metropolitan Museum of Art. The picture is *Japanese Robin and Chrysanthemums* by Kitagawa Utamaro (1754–1806) and is taken from *Momo-chidori,* an illustrated book of comic verse.

"Intermission": The phrase in italics is from *The Tempest* (IV. i).

"The Search": The phrase in italics is from Paul Celan's poem, "Psalm," in *Selected Poems and Prose of Paul Celan,* translated by John Felstiner (W. W. Norton, 2001).

"Cold Comfort": The epigraph is from Philippe Jaccottet, "March" (in *Three Fantasies*).

The back epigraph by Czeslaw Milosz is from the poem, "No More," translated by Anthony Milosz, in Czeslaw Milosz, *The Collected Poems* (Ecco Press, 1988).

EAMON GRENNAN was born in Dublin, Ireland, and divides his time between Poughkeepsie, New York, where he taught for many years at Vassar College, and the west of Ireland. He is the author of seven collections of poetry, including *The Quick of It* and *Still Life with Waterfall,* which won the 2003 Lenore Marshall Poetry Prize. He is also the author of *Facing the Music: Irish Poetry in the Twentieth Century* and the translator of *Leopardi: Selected Poems* and, with Rachel Kitzinger, *Oedipus at Colonus*. He continues to teach at New York University and Columbia University in New York.

The text of *Matter of Fact* is set in Sabon, an old-style serif typeface based on the types of Claude Garamond and designed by the German-born typographer and designer Jan Tschichold (1902–1974) in 1964. Book design by Ann Sudmeier. Composition at BookMobile Design and Publishing Services. Manufactured by Versa Press on acid-free paper.